All About Plants

All About

Roots

Claire Throp

capstone

Edited by Claire Throp and Brynn Baker
Designed by Peggie Carley
Picture research by Ruth Blair
Production by Victoria Fitzgerald
Originated by Capstone Global Library Ltd
Printed in the United States of America
009871RP

Library of Congress Cataloging-in-Publication Data

ISBN 978-1-4846-0508-0 (hardcover)
ISBN 978-1-4846-3848-4 (paperback)
ISBN 978-1-4846-0514-1 (ebook PDF)

Acknowledgments
We would like to thank the following for permission to reproduce photographs:

Corbis: Eye Ubiquitous/Michael Peuckert, 18; Getty Images: a.collectionRF/Yoshiharu Nuga, 20; Shutterstock: Adisorn Chaisan, 12, Anake Seenadee, 14, branislavpudar, 10, Christopher Elwell, 4, Denis and Yulia Pogostins, back cover, 17, 21, 23 (middle), Filipe B. Varela, 5, leungchopan, cover, Maljalen, 22, Maximus Art, 9, Olgysha, 13, Pavelk, 15, Peshkova, 6, Sergiy Bykhunenko, 16, 23 (top), siambizkit, 19, Sunny Forest, 7, Surakit, 11, winnond, 8, 23 (bottom)

We would like to thank Michael Bright for his invaluable help in the preparation of this book.

Every effort has been made to contact copyright holders of material reproduced in this book. Any omissions will be rectified in subsequent printings if notice is given to the publisher.

Contents

What Are Plants?

Plants are living things.

flower

stem

leaf

root

seed

Plants have
many parts.

What Do Plants Need to Grow?

Plants need sunlight and air to grow.

Plants need water to grow.

What Are Roots?

root

soil

Roots are one part of a plant.
Roots hold plants in the **soil**.

Roots take in water from the ground to help the plant grow.

Where Do Roots Grow?

Most roots grow underground.
We cannot see them.

Some roots grow above ground.

Some roots grow in the air.

Some roots grow into other plants.

Types of Roots

Young plants have small roots.

Old plants have big roots.

Some roots are **hairy**.

Some roots are **smooth**.

Some roots grow straight down.

Some roots spread out.

Roots as Food

People like to eat some roots.
Sweet potatoes are roots.

Carrots are roots too.

Plants Need Roots

Water moves through roots into the plant. Roots help the plant to grow.

Picture Glossary

 **hairy** covered in smaller, hair-like roots

 **smooth** free from rough or hairy roots

 **soil** top layer of earth where plants grow

Index

Notes for Parents and Teachers
Before Reading

Show children the roots of a plant. Ask them what they know about plant roots. Do they think all roots are the same?

After Reading

- Ask children if they can name some roots that we eat. Explain that some things we eat are stems rather than roots, but still grow under the ground. (potatoes)

- See if children can draw and label a whole plant without returning to the picture on page 5.

- Roots cannot always be seen, yet they are a very important part of a plant. Have children write two facts that support the following opinion: Roots are the most important part of a plant.